Science That's Appropriate <u>and</u> Doable

This science resource book was written with two goals in mind:

- to provide "good" science for your students
- to make it easy for you

What makes this book "good" science?

When you follow the step-by-step lessons in this book, you'll be using an instructional model that makes science education relevant to real life.

- Your students will be drawn in by interesting activities that encourage them to express what they already know about a concept.

- Your students will participate in hands-on discovery experiences and be guided to describe the experiences in their own words. Together, you'll record the experiences in both class and individual logbooks.

- You'll provide explanations and vocabulary that will help your students accurately explain what they have experienced.

- Your students will have opportunities to apply their new understandings to new situations.

What makes this book easy for you?

- The step-by-step activities are easy to understand and have illustrations where it's important.

- The resources you need are at your fingertips — record sheets; logbook forms; and other reproducibles such as minibooks, task cards, picture cards, and pages to make into overhead transparencies.

- Each science concept is presented in a self-contained section. You can decide to do the entire book or pick only those sections that enhance your own curriculum.

For sites on the World Wide Web that supplement the material in this resource book, go to http://www.evan-moor.com and look for the <u>Product Updates</u> link on the main page.

Using Logbooks as Learning Tools

Logbooks are valuable learning tools for several reasons:
- Logbooks give students an opportunity to put what they are learning into their own words.
- Putting ideas into words is an important step in internalizing new information. Whether spoken or written, this experience allows students to synthesize their thinking.
- Explaining and describing experiences help students make connections between several concepts and ideas.
- Logbook entries allow the teacher to catch misunderstandings right away and then reteach.
- Logbooks are a useful reference for students and a record of what has been learned.

Two Types of Logbooks

The Class Logbook

A class logbook is completed by the teacher and the class together. The teacher records student experiences and helps students make sense of their observations. The class logbook is a working document. You will return to it often for a review of what has been learned. As new information is acquired, make additions and corrections to the logbook.

Individual Science Logbooks

Individual students process their own understanding of investigations by writing their own responses in their own logbooks. Two types of logbook pages are provided in this unit.

1. Open-ended logbook pages:
   Pages 4 and 5 provide two choices of pages that can be used to respond to activities in the unit. At times you may wish students to write in their own logbooks and then share their ideas as the class logbook entry is made. After the class logbook has been completed, allow students to revise and add information to their own logbooks. At other times you may wish students to copy the class logbook entry into their own logbooks.

2. Specific logbook pages:
   You will find record forms or activity sheets following many activities that can be added to each student's logbook.

At the conclusion of the unit, reproduce a copy of the logbook cover on page 3 for each student. Students can then organize both types of pages and staple them with the cover.

_____'s
Energy Log

Note: Reproduce this form for students to record knowledge gained during daily science lessons.

Name _____

This is what I learned about energy today:

Note: Reproduce this form for students to record science investigations.

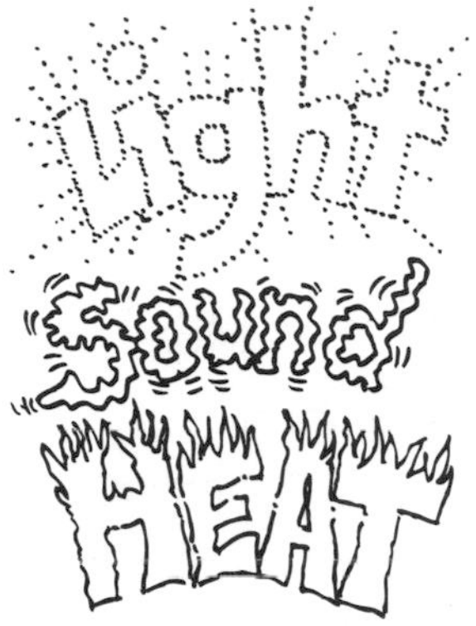

Name ______________________________

Investigation: ______________________________

What we did:

____

____

____

What we saw:

____

____

____

What we learned:

____

____

____

Energy can move and change things.

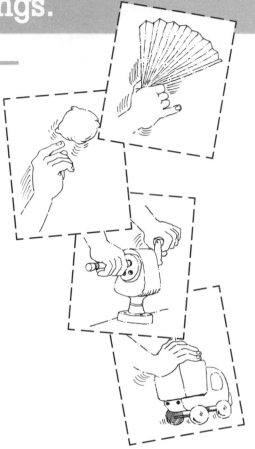

Thinking about Moving Things

Materials

- bean bag
- small fan or paper folded into fan
- toy car or truck
- pencil sharpener
- pencil
- picture cards on page 9

Steps to Follow

1. Direct students to complete the following tasks:
   Throw the bean bag to a friend.
   Cool a classmate with the fan.
   Push the toy across the floor.
   Sharpen a pencil.

2. Show the picture cards one at a time and ask:
   Is something moving in the picture?
   What made it move?

   Record student responses on a class logbook page entitled "Moving Things."

- Have students create a list of things that move. Record their ideas on a large chart. Read over the chart. Talk about similarities and differences among the items listed.

  Ask questions to help students realize that all moving things have some force that is causing their motion.
  Have you ever seen a (motorcycle) when it wasn't moving? What changed to make it move?

- Reproduce page 4 for each student to write a page for his or her individual logbook. Students are to finish this sentence and give some examples:

  Anything that moves has....
  (a force that causes the motion, something pushing it.)

Moving Things

The bean bag is moving.

John's hand lifted the bean bag and pushed it through the air.

- If students haven't already defined the force that causes motion as energy, supply the term for them. Papa Bear in *The Berenstain's Bears Science Fair* (Random House, 1977) describes energy as "the go of things." Create your own class definition for energy and post it. For example, "Energy is the force that makes things move."

- Reproduce page 10 for students. Have students identify the moving object and then describe what is causing the movement. (They are identifying the energy sources.)

- Reproduce page 11 for students. Students will take the record sheet home and identify four different moving things. They will draw the things, name the things, and identify the sources of energy. Discuss the pages when they are returned.

Changes You Can See

These activities can be done in small groups, in a center, or as demonstrations with the whole class participating.

Reproduce three copies of the logbook form on page 5 for each student. Students will record their observations. Their writing should reflect the fact that changes occurred to the ice cube, the cream, and the bread.

Melt It

ice cube
clear glass bowl

1. Set the bowl with the ice cube in it in a sunny spot.
2. Have different students observe what happens over time.

Making Butter

baby food jars with lids
heavy cream

1. Pour 1/3 cup of cream into each jar.
2. Secure the lid.
3. Shake until cream changes to a solid.

Toast It

toaster
slices of bread

1. Put bread in toaster.
2. Watch what happens.

Follow Up

Ask students to tell about the changes they observed and wrote about. What made the changes happen?

Through questioning, lead students to the understanding that energy caused the changes they observed. In the case of the ice cube, the energy was heat from sunlight; the cream changed due to movement caused by muscle energy; the toast was changed by heat energy from electricity.

• Write a class logbook page entitled "Things Energy Can Do." Add to the chart as additional information is gathered throughout this unit.

Things Energy Can Do

Energy moves things:
Balls
Fans
Toy cars
Pencil sharpeners

Energy changes things:
Ice to water
Cream to butter
Bread to toast
Dull pencils to sharp pencils

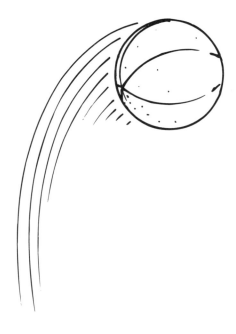

Note: Reproduce these picture cards for "Thinking about Moving Things" on page 6.

Note: Reproduce this page to follow up "Thinking about Moving Things" on page 7.

Name _____

What Made It Move?

Circle the moving thing in each picture.
Then tell what is making it move.

What's moving?

_____

Source of energy:

_____

What's moving?

_____

Source of energy:

_____

What's moving?

_____

Source of energy:

_____

What's moving?

_____

Source of energy:

_____

Name _____

Moving Things at My House

Draw

What moved?

_____

What made it move?

_____

Draw

What moved?

_____

What made it move?

_____

Draw

What moved?

_____

What made it move?

_____

Draw

What moved?

_____

What made it move?

_____

Energy: Light, Heat, & Sound • EMC 861

Energy exists in different forms.

Recognizing Energy

Energy in the Morning

- Make a transparency of the pictures on page 14. Show the transparency as you read this poem describing energy in the morning.

  Picture 1   BRRRING!
  My alarm goes off at eight.
  I'll hurry so I won't be late.

  Picture 2   I'm out of bed and in the shower.
  School will start in just one hour.

  Picture 3   Time for breakfast. Brush and comb.
  I'll clean up when I get home.

  Picture 4   Grab my lunch and pat the cat.
  I'm off for school, just like that!

- Let students describe their own morning routines. Refer to the class definition of energy. Ask them if they used energy during their early morning. List responses on a class logbook page entitled "Energy in Our Mornings." Ask students to think about whether all the energy was from the same source.

Energy in the Classroom

Materials

copies of Energy Expert Recording Sheets (page 15)

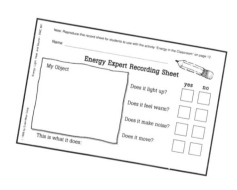

Steps to Follow

1. Students choose a classroom object that moves.
2. They follow directions on the sheet to draw and analyze their objects.

Follow Up

When individual findings have been reported, discuss the findings in general. Guide the discussion with questions like these:

"Do all of the objects do the same thing?"
"Do all of the objects move?"
"Do all of the objects change other things?"
"What do these objects have to do with energy?"
"Do all of the objects need energy?"

Categorizing Energy

Three Kinds of Energy

Materials

- picture cards from pages 16–17
- yarn or rope
- energy labels from page 18

Steps to Follow

1. Make three large overlapping circles on the floor.
2. Explain that scientists recognize light, heat, and sound as three different kinds of energy.
3. Label the circles Light, Heat, and Sound.
4. Show a picture card. Discuss whether the picture represents light, heat, or sound energy or a combination of different kinds of energy. Accept any answers that can be justified. *(The stove definitely represents heat energy, but as the burners or flames get hot, they glow. So they also represent light energy.)*
5. Put the cards in the appropriate section of the Venn diagram to show the kind(s) of energy.

HEAT ENERGY

SOUND ENERGY

LIGHT ENERGY

Different Kinds of Energy in the School

Check students' understanding as you ask them to label heat, light, and sound energy in the school.

Materials

- 3" x 5" (7.5 x 13 cm) index cards
- masking tape

Steps to Follow

Divide students into small groups.

1. Give each group 6 index cards. They are to write Heat Energy on two cards, Light Energy on two cards, and Sound Energy on two cards. Send each group to a different part of the school.
2. Students attach the labels to things that represent the three kinds of energy.

Note: Make a transparency of these pictures to use with the activity "Energy in the Morning" on page 12.

Energy in the Morning

Note: Reproduce this record sheet for students to use with the activity "Energy in the Classroom" on page 12.

Name ____

Energy Expert Recording Sheet

My Object

	yes	no
Does it light up?	☐	☐
Does it feel warm?	☐	☐
Does it make noise?	☐	☐
Does it move?	☐	☐

This is what it does:

____

- -

Name ____

Energy Expert Recording Sheet

My Object:

	yes	no
Does it light up?	☐	☐
Does it feel warm?	☐	☐
Does it make noise?	☐	☐
Does it move?	☐	☐

This is what it does:

____

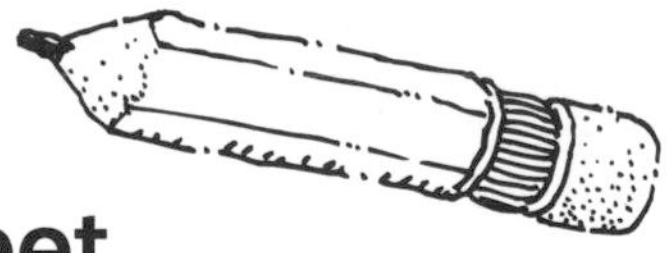

Note: Reproduce these energy signs to label the sections of the Venn diagram in the activity on page 13.

HEAT ENERGY

- -

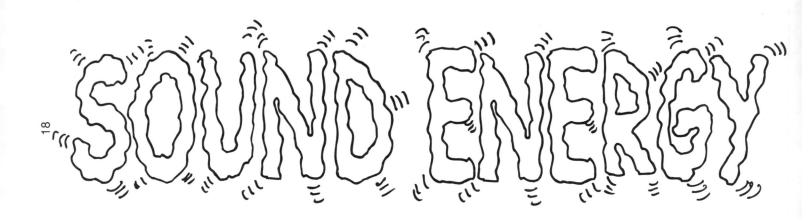

SOUND ENERGY

- -

LIGHT ENERGY

Light is energy you can see.

Exploring Light Energy

Exploration 1—Where Does Our Light Come From?

Make an overhead transparency of the poster on page 21. Show the transparency and ask students to describe the different light energy sources in the poster.

Exploration 2 — A Light Walk

Take your class on a light walk. Identify all the places that light comes from in your school environment. Be sure to walk both indoors and outdoors so that students will see both natural and man-made light sources.

When you return to the classroom, create a list on a class logbook page entitled "Light Sources We Use." Encourage students to add light sources that they have experienced outside of the school environment.

Light Sources We Use

the sun
lamps
ceiling lights
headlights on cars
candles
kerosene lanterns

Exploration 3 — Light Energy At Home

Reproduce the record sheet on page 22 for individual students. Have them find 4 different kinds of lights at their houses.

Kinds of Light

• Explain that the place that light comes from is called a light source. Light can come from a natural source like the sun or the stars. Light can also come from a man-made or artificial source like a lamp or a candle.

Reproduce the activity sheet on page 23 and discuss whether the light sources pictured are natural or man-made.

• Have students classify the light sources from their homework record sheet (page 22) as man-made or natural.

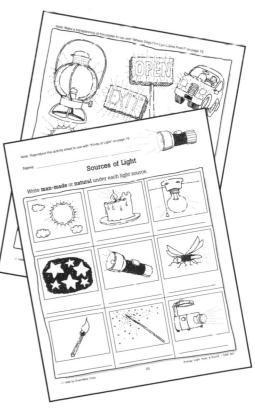

       Energy: Light, Heat, & Sound • EMC 861

Gather More Information

- There are several excellent trade books about lighthouses. Read one of them to your class and discuss the source of light in the lighthouse.

  Beacons of Light: Lighthouses by Gail Gibbons; Scholastic, 1996.
  Birdie's Lighthouse by Deborah Hopkinson; Atheneum Books, 1997.

- Invite a photographer to come to your classroom and talk about how photographs are developed. Discover the important part light energy plays in the process.

Extension Activity—Light Can Change Things

Students will see a vivid example of how light can change things when they create light prints with blueprint paper.

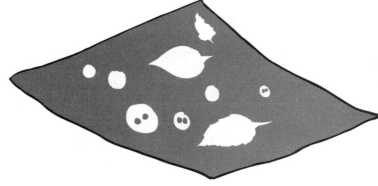

Materials

- 3" x 4" (7.5 x 10 cm) piece of blueprint paper
- piece of glass large enough to cover the paper
- small leaves
- coins, shells, and buttons
- used file folders or pieces of cardboard

Steps to Follow

1. Place the blueprint paper on a folder or piece of cardboard for easy carrying.
2. Arrange a few of the small objects on the blueprint paper.
3. Put the clear glass on top of the objects to hold them in place.
4. Place the paper in the direct sun for several seconds.
5. Remove the objects and wash the paper with cold water.
6. Note the changes that the light energy has made.

The blueprint paper is covered with chemicals that are sensitive to light. The chemicals dissolve in water. When the light strikes the chemicals a new bright blue chemical is formed. The blueprint paper under the leaf is not exposed to light and so it remains white.

Note: Make a transparency of this poster to use with "Where Does Our Light Come From?" on page 19.

Day or night
We need light!

Energy: Light, Heat, & Sound • EMC 861

Name _____

Light Energy at My House

light source:

draw

where I found it:

_____

light source:

draw

where I found it:

_____

light source:

draw

where I found it:

_____

light source:

draw

where I found it:

_____

Note: Reproduce this activity sheet to use with "Kinds of Light" on page 19.

Name _____

Sources of Light

Write **man-made** or **natural** under each light source.

Energy: Light, Heat, & Sound • EMC 861

Light moves in a straight line.

Exploring How Light Moves

Exploration 1—Where Will the Light Go?

Do this activity with your students to draw upon their previous experiences with light energy.

Materials

flashlight(s)

Steps to Follow

1. Four students stand at the front of the room.
2. Teacher stands at the back of the room with a flashlight.
3. Point the flashlight at one student's chest. Ask students to predict where the light will go.
4. Have a helper turn the room lights off. Turn the flashlight on.

Follow Up

Were the predictions correct? How could the class predict where the light would go?

Repeat several times.

Exploration 2 — In a Straight Line

Materials

- 3 index cards
- 3 small blocks of wood
- tape or stapler
- flashlight
- a piece of black construction paper
- pile of books

Preparation

1. Make a hole, about the size of a quarter, in the center of three index cards.
2. Tack each card to a small block of wood.
3. Place the index cards and blocks six inches apart in a straight line.
   (It's easier to line the holes up if you work in the dark and use a flashlight.)
4. Balance a flashlight on a pile of books about three feet from the first card. Adjust the height of the pile of books so that the light shines directly through the holes.

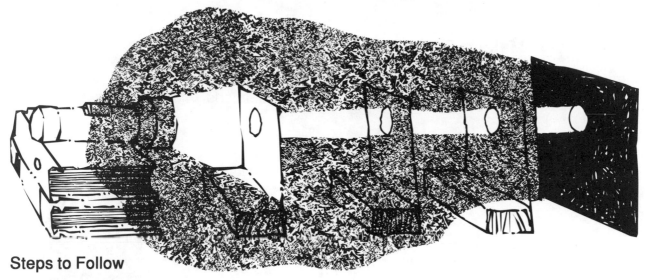

Steps to Follow

1. Darken the room.
2. Hold the black paper in back of the last index card.
3. Turn on the flashlight.

Does the light shine through all three cards onto the black paper?
What does that show about how light travels?

> Clapping chalky erasers over the cards as
> you shine the light through will make the
> beam of light more visible.

4. Turn off the flashlight. Move one card out of line and have
   students predict what will happen when the light is turned on.
5. Check predictions by turning the flashlight back on.

Follow Up

• Reproduce the activity sheet on page 27 for individual students.
  Have students draw the rays of light in each picture.

• Have students generalize about how light moves. Record
  their observations on a class logbook page entitled "We Can
  See Light Move."

We Can See Light Move

Light shines through holes.

Light moves in a straight line.

Extension Activity—Make a Super Viewer

The super viewer is a great way to see light moving in a straight line. For younger students, make one super viewer to be used in a light center and for demonstrations. Older students may want to make their own viewers.

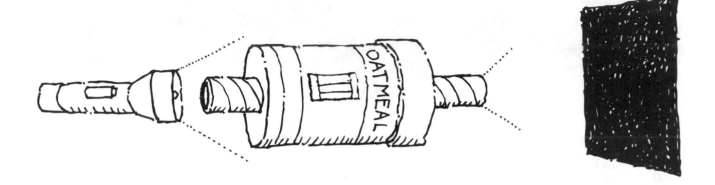

Materials

- oatmeal box
- two toilet paper tubes
- masking tape
- black paint
- plastic wrap
- flashlight

To Make the Viewer

1. Paint the insides of the oatmeal box and the tubes with black paint. Let them dry.
2. Make a hole in the center of each end panel of the oatmeal box.
3. Put a toilet paper tube into each of the holes. Tape the tubes so that they can't slip.
4. Tape over any holes or cracks that you find in the box.
5. Cut a small window in the side of the box.
6. Cover the window with a piece of plastic wrap and tape it in place.

Using the Viewer

In a dark room:
1. Hold a black paper just beyond one tube.
2. Point the flashlight through the end of the other tube.
3. Turn the flashlight on.
4. Have students predict what they will see when they peek through the window in the side of the tube to see the beam of light.
5. Students should check their predictions and record their observations using the form on page 5.

Note: Reproduce this activity sheet to use with "In a Straight Line" on page 25.

Name _____

Show How It Moves

Draw rays of light from each light source to show how the light will move.

Light can pass through some materials and is stopped by other materials.

How Much Light Passes Through?

• Hold up three cups — one glass; one colored, translucent plastic; and one Styrofoam®. Place the cups on a table so that students can see the sides of the cups, but can not look in the tops. Fill the cups with different amounts of colored water.

Ask students to tell which cup contains the most water. Record their reactions on a class logbook page entitled "What Can You See?"

• Create a center where students can test materials to determine how much light passes through. You may want to model how this is done before asking individuals to work on their own. Be sure to include materials that are transparent, translucent, and opaque. (Don't use these terms yet.)

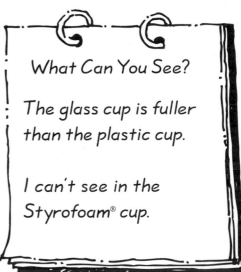

What Can You See?

The glass cup is fuller than the plastic cup.

I can't see in the Styrofoam® cup.

Materials

• record sheet on page 30
• items for designing the test: flashlight, black paper, window, lamp, box
• items to test: cardboard, foil, a towel, a plastic bowl, cellophane, tissue paper, muslin, waxed paper, a china plate, a mirror, a metal pie pan, a piece of wood, a ceramic tile, clear acetate, a clear plastic cup, a cardboard box, a clipboard

Steps to Follow

1. Design a test to rate materials on the amount of light that passes through them. Describe the test on the record sheet. Example:

   I will hold each object up to the lamp and judge the amount of light that shines through it.
   I will shine a flashlight toward an object while I hold a black paper in back of the object.

2. Test each of the objects.
3. Sort the items tested into groups representing the test results.
4. Give names to the groups and record test results on the record sheet.

Follow Up

• After the students have classified the materials individually, talk about the results by asking questions:

> "How did you group the materials?"
> "What are the attributes of each group?"

If students fail to focus on the differences in the amount of light that passes through different materials, ask:

> "What kinds of materials let a lot of light pass through?"
> "What kinds of materials let no light pass through?"
> "What kinds of materials let some light pass through?"

• Inform students that:
> Materials that let a lot of light pass through are called **transparent**.
> Materials that let no light pass through are called **opaque**.
> Materials that let some light pass through are called **translucent**.

Have students compare these three categories with their material groups.

Challenge students to find other materials that would fit in a transparent group, a translucent group, and an opaque group. Add those materials to your sorting center.

• Reproduce the activity sheet on page 31. Have students fill in the blanks to answer the questions and justify their answers.

Review the sheets in a class discussion and talk about why it is important to control light by using materials that it can't pass through. Consider products like windows, shades, sunglasses, and visors.

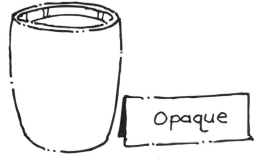

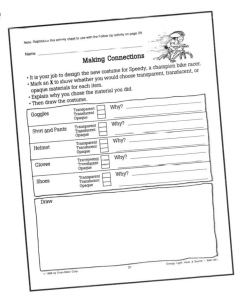

Note: Reproduce this record sheet for use with "How Much Light Passes Through?" on page 28.

Name ______________________________

How Much Light?

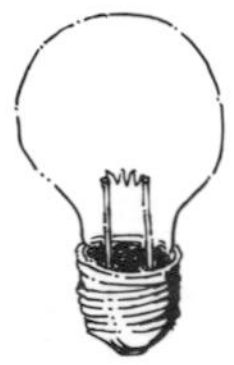

Your job is to test objects to see how much light shines through them.
Think of a test. Describe the test you will do.

____

____

____

Now test the objects.
Sort the objects into groups by the amount of light that shines through them.
Give each group a descriptive name and write the names below.
Write the name of each item in the group where it belongs.

Group 1 Name:	Group 2 Name:	Group 3 Name:

Note: Reproduce this activity sheet to use with the Follow Up activity on page 29.

Name ______________________________

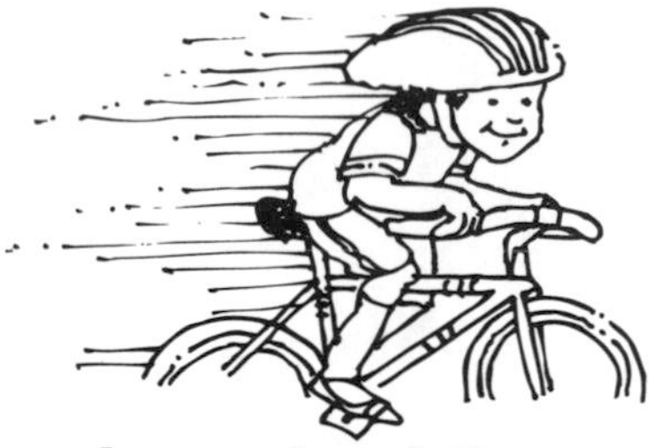

Making Connections

- It is your job to design the new costume for Speedy, a champion bike racer.
- Mark an **X** to show whether you would choose transparent, translucent, or opaque materials for each item.
- Explain why you chose the material you did.
- Then draw the costume.

Goggles	Transparent ☐ Translucent ☐ Opaque ☐	Why?	
Shirt and Pants	Transparent ☐ Translucent ☐ Opaque ☐	Why?	
Helmet	Transparent ☐ Translucent ☐ Opaque ☐	Why?	
Gloves	Transparent ☐ Translucent ☐ Opaque ☐	Why?	
Shoes	Transparent ☐ Translucent ☐ Opaque ☐	Why?	

Draw

Light can be controlled by blocking a light source.

Changing Shadows

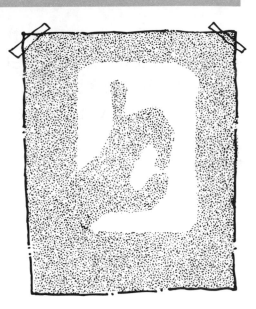

Materials

- large piece of newsprint
- filmstrip projector
- logbook form on page 4

Steps to Follow

1. Tape a large piece of newsprint on one wall of your classroom.
2. Set up a projector so that its light shines on the paper.
3. Let all students have a chance to make a shadow in front of the light. (Warn students that looking straight at the light can hurt their eyes.) Encourage observers to notice how shadows change as students move.

Follow Up

- Use the logbook page for students to write about making shadows. If needed, provide this starter: When I made a shadow I...
- If your students have had little experience with shadows, try this:
  Turn off the projector. One at a time, ask students to stand in various places — some within the rays of the light and some outside. Have the other students predict whether a shadow will be cast. Turn on the projector to verify. Have students explain why sometimes there is a shadow and sometimes there is none.

  (To have a shadow, the object must block the light.)

A Shadow Center

Materials

- familiar objects from the classroom, kitchen, and/or workshop
- light source — a flashlight, a lamp without a shade, or a projector
- good-sized pieces of newsprint
- crayons
- Shadow Center Activity cards on page 33
- masking tape

Form pairs of students to explore the center. Students will choose an object and explore that object's shadows by completing the jobs on Shadow Center Activity 1. After all students have completed Shadow Activity 1, rotate them back through the center to do Shadow Center Activity 2.

Energy: Light, Heat, and Sound • EMC 861

Shadow Center Activity 1

• Tape a sheet of paper onto the wall.

• Hold your object in front of the light source so that its shadow hits the paper on the wall.

• Turn the object slowly.
   Does the shadow change? How? Talk about it with your partner.

• Move the object close to the light and farther away.
   Does the shadow change? How?
   Which shadow looks most like the object?
   Talk about it with your partner.

• Choose one shadow that is particularly interesting. Draw around the interesting shadow with a crayon. Take down the paper.

• Label the drawing with your names.

Shadow Center Activity 2

Match the objects used in Shadow Activity 1 to the shadow drawings.

• Lay out the drawings and lay the objects on top until you find a match.

• Record your matches on another sheet of paper. For example:

   Todd and Jeremy's shadow — potato masher
   Sarah and Jon's shadow — wire whisk

Energy: Light, Heat, and Sound • EMC 861

Summary Activities

• Read *Bear Shadow* by Frank Asch (Prentice Hall, 1985).
Your students will love knowing more about shadows than
Bear does.

Write class or individual letters to Bear explaining what
caused his shadow. (Individual letters will serve as a good
check for understanding.)

• On a sunny day go for a walk to search for shadows. As
shadows are seen, ask these questions:
    "What is making the shadow?"
    "Why is there a shadow?" *(an object is blocking the sun's light)*

Take your computer camera with you on the walk. When you
see an interesting shadow, take a photo. When the pictures
are downloaded, have students compose captions. Each
caption should identify
    the light source,
    the light blocker, and
    the place where the shadow was found.
Print the pages to make a Shadow Journal.

Heat is energy you can feel.

Sources of Heat

- Reproduce the picture cards on page 37. (You might want to copy them as a transparency.) Show the four pictures and ask students to explain what the four objects have in common. (Student responses will vary, but should include the idea that all produce heat.)

- Have students list as many sources of heat as they can. This can be done in small groups or as a class activity. Record the ideas on a class logbook page entitled "Heat Producers."

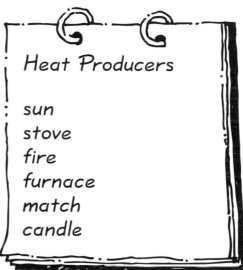

Heat Producers

sun
stove
fire
furnace
match
candle

Feeling Heat

Students rotate through four stations to experience feeling different forms of heat — warm water, electric heat, and friction.

Heat Task 3
Lay your hand on a heating pad or hot-water bottle. Write about what happens.

Heat Task 1
Dip your hand into warm water. Write about what happens.

- Give each student a copy of the record sheet on page 39 on which to record observations following each experience.

- Divide students into pairs or small groups to share their observations. Listen during the sharing for words indicating that they felt heat. (You may wish to introduce the term "friction.") Help students conclude that heat is something you feel.

Thermometers Measure Heat

- Ask students to explain how heat is measured. If students are not familiar with thermometer use, introduce the thermometer as a tool that measures heat. Bring examples of several different types of thermometers to class and demonstrate their use.

- Make an overhead transparency of the directions on page 40 to make a simple thermometer. Follow the directions together to make one thermometer to be used in the class.

- Demonstrate the use of the thermometer you made with these two experiments. Each student will need two copies of the logbook form on page 5.

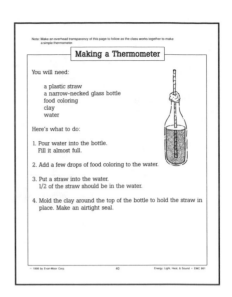

Experiment 1

Put your thermometer in a deep pan.
Pour hot water into the pan.
Watch the water in the straw.
Write about what you see happen.

Experiment 2

Put your thermometer in a deep pan.
Pour cold water into the pan.
Watch the water in the straw.
Write about what you see happen.

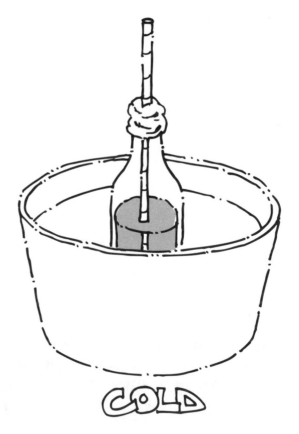

Note: Reproduce these picture cards to use with page 35.

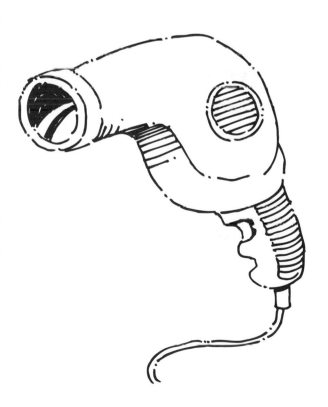

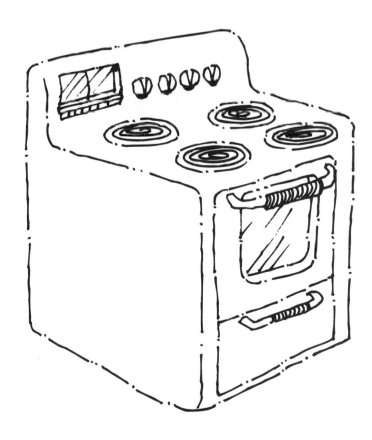

 Energy: Light, Heat, & Sound • EMC 861

Heat Task 1

Dip your hand into warm water.
Write about what happens.

Heat Task 2

Rub your hands together for a minute.
Write about what happens.

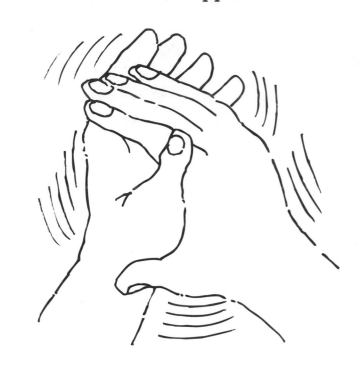

Heat Task 3

Lay your hand on a heating pad
or hot-water bottle.
Write about what happens.

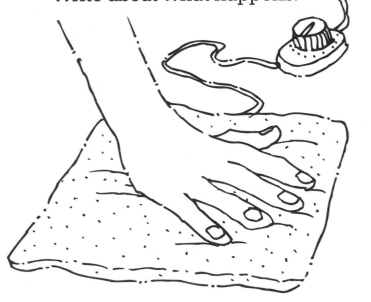

Heat Task 4

Sand a block of wood with a piece
of sandpaper.
Write about what happens.

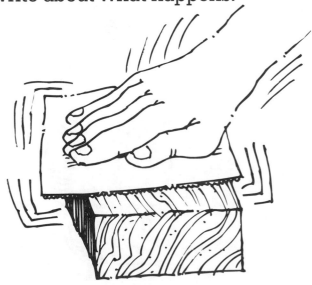

Name _____

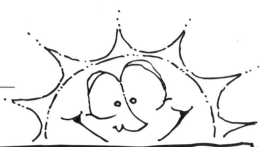

Feeling Heat

Heat Task 1

What I did...

_____

_____

What I felt...

_____

_____

_____

Heat Task 2

What I did...

_____

_____

What I felt...

_____

_____

_____

Heat Task 3

What I did...

_____

_____

What I felt...

_____

_____

_____

Heat Task 4

What I did...

_____

_____

What I felt...

_____

_____

_____

Making a Thermometer

You will need:

    a plastic straw
    a narrow-necked glass bottle
    food coloring
    clay
    water

Here's what to do:

1. Pour water into the bottle.
   Fill it almost full.

2. Add a few drops of food coloring to the water.

3. Put a straw into the water.
   1/2 of the straw should be in the water.

4. Mold the clay around the top of the bottle to hold the straw in place. Make an airtight seal.

 Energy: Light, Heat, & Sound • EMC 861

Heat can cause things to move or change.

Heat Can Cause Things to Move

Divide your class into pairs or small groups to brew tea.
Reproduce the record sheet on page 44 for every student.

Materials (for each group)

- 2 clear glass jars
- 2 tea bags
- labels for jars
- hot water
- cold water
- brown crayons
- pencils
- kitchen timer

Steps to Follow

1. Label one jar "Hot" and one jar "Cold."
2. Pour hot water in the "Hot" jar and cold water in the "Cold" jar.
   (This may be a job for the teacher or an adult helper.)
3. Add a tea bag to each jar.
4. Set the timer for two minutes.
5. When the timer is finished, draw and write to tell what happened. Do the two jars look alike or different?
6. Set the timer for another two minutes.
7. When the timer is finished, compare the two jars again. Write and draw to tell about any differences.

Follow Up

Have students report the results of their observations. Ask them to speculate about why they think differences may have occurred. (The molecules in the hot water are moving faster and so they mix more quickly with the tea than the molecules in the cold water. Eventually, by the time the water in both jars reach room temperature, the tea will look the same in both.)

Think about it — Why does Timmy's mother make tea by putting a jar of water and tea bags out in the sun?

Heat Can Cause Things to Change

Make Popcorn

Bring an air popper to class and pop some popcorn. Have students use the logbook form on page 5 to record the changes. Ask, "What causes the kernels to pop (change)?"
(The water molecules inside the kernels move faster and farther apart as they are heated. Finally, the kernel can not contain this energy and the kernel bursts.)

Everyday Changes

• Reproduce the activity sheet on page 45 for individual students. You may want to make a transparency to guide the class discussion as students look at their own sheets.

• Ask students to describe the beach scene.
(The boy is sitting on a beach chair. His wet towel is dumped at the end of the chair. He has an icy cold drink in his hand and his sandwich is on a plate beside the chair.)

Ask them to infer what the weather must be like.
(Since the sun is shining and the boy is drinking something cold, it must be hot.)

• Have students write about the picture to describe any changes that the heat might cause. Do the activity as a class or write one statement on the transparency as a model and ask students to complete the activity. *(The boy might get sunburned. The sandwich bread will get hard. The ice in the lemonade will melt. The towel will dry out.)*

Make a Bubble without Blowing

Materials

- dishwashing detergent
- small metal can with one end removed
- flat plate
- logbook form on page 5

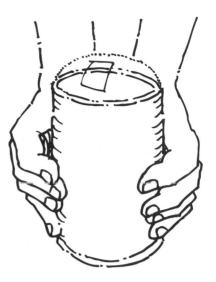

Steps to Follow

1. Put the metal can in the refrigerator or in an ice chest to cool it off. A cold can works best.
2. Make a bubble mixture from water and a small amount of dishwashing detergent. Pour the mixture onto the plate.
3. Dip the open end of the cold can into the bubble mixture.
4. Turn the can upright. There should be bubble film covering the opening. If not, dip the can into the bubble mixture again.
5. Put your hands around the can and hold tightly.
6. Watch what happens. Have students write their observations on logbook pages.

Have some extra cans cooling for faster retries.

Follow Up

As students share results of this activity, ask:

"What caused the change in the bubble film?"

(As the air inside the can warmed up, the molecules moved faster and took up more space. When the air tried to move out of the can, it pushed against the bubble film and made a bubble.)

"Where did the heat come from?

(the warm hands on the cold can)

Help students generalize that heat energy can cause changes.

 Energy: Light, Heat, & Sound • EMC 861

Note: Reproduce this record sheet to use with the activity on page 41.

Name ____

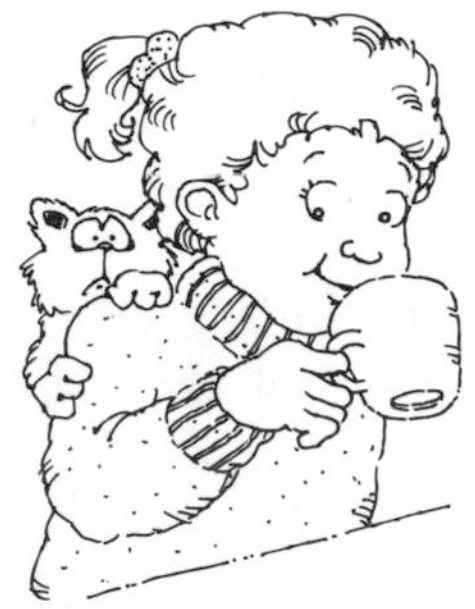

Brewing Tea

Draw and write to show what happened.

Before the tea bag was added:

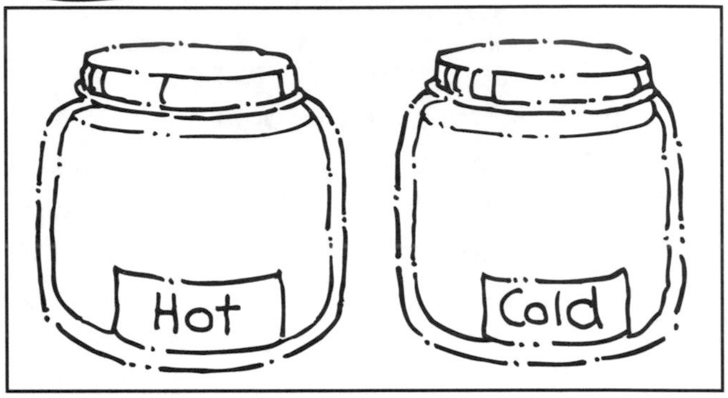

What I saw: ______________________

____

____

After two minutes:

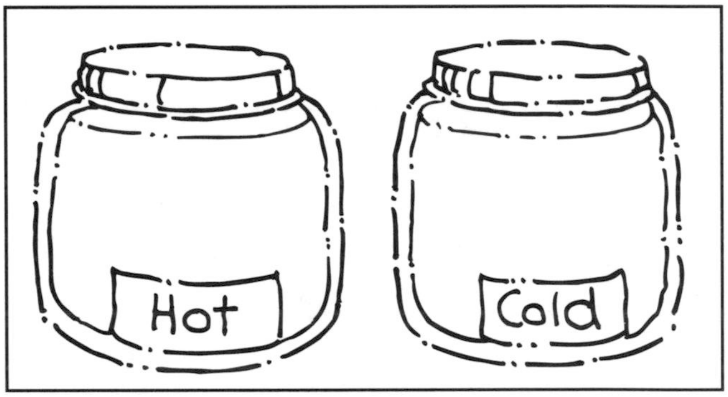

What I saw: ______________________

____

____

After four minutes:

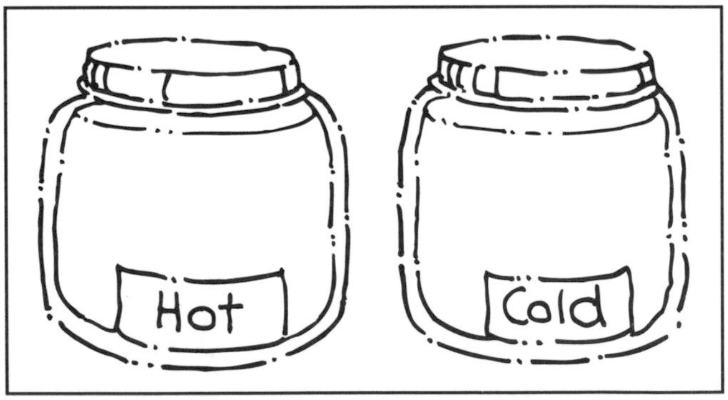

What I saw: ______________________

____

____

Why I think this happened:

____

____

Note: Reproduce this page to use with page 42.

Heat Causes Changes

Tell about the changes that will happen here.

_____

_____

_____

_____

 Energy: Light, Heat, & Sound • EMC 861

Heat travels from warm objects to cold ones.

Heat Travels—Demonstration 1

Materials

- metal knitting needle or a straightened metal clothes hanger
- candle wax
- thumbtacks
- candle
- logbook form on page 5

Steps to Follow

1. Before the activity fasten the thumbtacks at intervals along the knitting needle by dripping candle wax from a burning candle onto the rod and holding the tacks in the wax until it hardens.

2. Hold the knitting needle with a potholder.

3. Put the other end of the needle in a candle flame. Ask students to predict what will happen.

4. Watch the wax and the thumbtacks. Ask questions about what causes the wax to melt:
   "Is there a pattern in the way the wax melts and drops the tacks?"
   "How can the pattern be explained?"
   "How is the heat moving?"

Follow Up

Record student observations on a class logbook page entitled "Heat Travelers" and have students complete individual logbook pages, using the form on page 5.

Heat Travels

Heat travels through the metal.

The tacks fall off in order.

The tack closest to the heat falls off first.

Heat Travels—Demonstration 2

Divide the class into small groups so everyone can feel what happens to the spoons.

Materials (for each group)

- hot soup or hot water
- bowl
- metal spoon
- plastic spoon
- wooden spoon (wooden craft sticks or ice-cream spoons can be used— spoons should be approximately the same size)

Steps to Follow

1. Feel the three spoons. Note any difference in the temperature.
2. Pour the hot liquid into a bowl.
3. Put the three spoons into the liquid.
4. Hold the handles of the spoons. Tell about any changes you notice.

Follow Up

- Record observations on a class logbook page entitled "Cool Spoons in Hot Liquid."
- Reproduce the logbook form on page 5. Have students write about what they did and what they felt, being sure to tell which spoon got hot faster than the others. Challenge students to explain why they think there was a difference.

Cool Spoons In Hot Liquid

The metal spoon gets hot fast.

The wooden spoon stays cool.

The plastic spoon stays cool.

Heat Minibook

- Reproduce pages 48–50. Cut the pages in half and staple them together to form student booklets. Read the booklet with your students. Help them to connect their knowledge about how heat moves with the common experiences described in the booklet.
- Extend the learning experience by having students think of more examples of heat moving from a hot thing to a cooler thing and then writing additional pages for the book.

Check for Understanding

Reproduce the quiz on page 51. Have students draw the arrows and write sentences to show which way the heat will move. Review the student responses and correct any misconceptions.

Name _____

Heat

Heat warms our homes and us. It cooks your breakfast. It helps flowers grow.

Heat is used to do work. In factories, heat helps to make things that we use every day.

1

Heat can move.

Heat makes things move. It makes a train engine go and sends a rocket into outer space. It makes jets soar into the sky and cars speed down freeways.

2

Heat moves from warm places to colder places.

One of the laws of nature is that all things want to go to their lowest energy levels. Objects give up their heat in order to give up their energy. If a warm object touches a cooler object, its heat will go directly to the cool object.

3

Heat from the sun moves to the snow and the snow melts.

The sun is the most important source of heat for the earth. Heat waves from the sun travel 93 million miles to the earth. This kind of movement is called **radiation** or radiant heat.

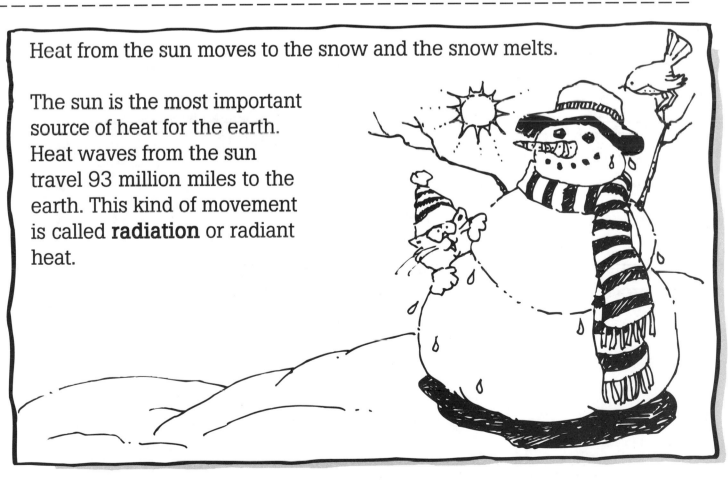

4

Heat from the stove moves from the burner to the pan to the cold soup and warms it up.

The process of transferring heat from molecule to molecule is called **conduction**. Metals are better **conductors** of heat because the molecules in metal are close together. Plastics are bad conductors of heat so they make good handles for pots and pans. Bad conductors of heat are called **insulators**.

5

Heat from the campfire moves to my cold hands and I feel warmer.

The fire heats the air right above it and makes the molecules in the air move around very fast and take up more space. The hot air rises. When heated matter moves from one place to another, the process is called **convection**.

6

Note: Reproduce this page to use with "Check for Understanding" on page 47.

Name _____

Which Way Will It Move?

Draw an arrow to show which way the heat will move. Then write a sentence to tell about the moving.

a warm house

a cold winter

cookie dough

a hot oven

a cold man

hot water

Energy: Light, Heat, & Sound • EMC 861

Heat can be controlled by containing it.

Think about Controlling Heat

- Show students a blanket, a thermos bottle, and a tea cozy, or use the picture cards on page 55. Ask them to tell the purpose of each item and to explain how each item works.

  Reproduce the logbook form on page 4 and have students write in response to the question:
    "How can containing heat energy help you?"

- Make an overhead transparency of page 56 and show it to students as you read the poem. Ask students to explain why the child is happy.

  Ask students to describe how they keep warm. Write suggestions on a class logbook page entitled "How We Keep Warm."

How We Keep Warm

I wear a sweatshirt over my T-shirt.

I wear two pairs of socks.

I wear a hat on my head.

Energy: Light, Heat, & Sound • EMC 861

Controlling Heat to Keep It Hot

Mrs. Check's Problem

Make a transparency of the picture of Mrs. Check on page 57.

Introduce Mrs. Check to your class and explain her problem about keeping her coffee hot by telling this story:

Note: Make a transparency of this picture to use with page 53.

Meet Mrs. Check

© 1998 by Evan-Moor Corp.   57   Energy: Light, Heat, & Sound • EMC 861

Mrs. Check works in the library at school. Every morning when she gets to school, she fills her cup with hot coffee. She loves hot coffee.

All the teachers hurry into the library to find books to help their students learn. Mrs. Check loves helping teachers find just the right book.

All the students hurry into the library to find new books for projects, to help them solve problems, and just for reading. Mrs. Check loves helping students find just the book they need.

The phone rings, the computer beeps, and the fax machine whirs. Mrs. Check answers the phone, works on the computer, and delivers a fax. Mrs. Check loves being busy.

What a morning! Mrs. Check takes a sip of her coffee. ICK!! The coffee is cold. Mrs. Check does not love cold coffee.

There is a real Mrs. Check (only it's spelled Cech), and she does have trouble finding time to drink her coffee before it gets cold.

A Class Project

Bring a thermos of hot coffee or hot water to class. Ask students, "Can we think of a way to help Mrs. Check keep her coffee hot so that she can enjoy it after she does all the things she loves doing?"

As a class think of ways to control the heat. Record the suggestions on a class logbook page entitled "Keeping the Heat in a Cup of Coffee."

Choose one suggestion and test it. For example:
Suggestion: Cover the cup of coffee with a paper.
    Test: Check the temperature of two cups of coffee (or hot water) — one uncovered and one covered with a paper — after 5, 10, and 15 minutes.

Record the results of the test on a chart similar to the following.

Keeping the Heat in a Cup of Coffee

Put the cup on the stove.

Put a lid on the cup.

Wrap the cup with a towel.

	temperature of a cup of coffee covered with a paper	temperature of a cup of coffee uncovered
After 5 minutes		
After 10 minutes		
After 15 minutes		

A Small Group Project

Challenge small groups of students to test their own "heat controllers" against a control cup. You will provide cups (2 per group), thermometers (2 per group), hot water, and the record form on page 58.

In an initial session, groups meet to plan their test and draw up a list of materials and outline the jobs that each person will do. You may want students to bring test materials from home or to give you their lists so that you can provide the materials.

After the groups have conducted their tests and completed their record sheets, share each project with the whole class.

Check for Understanding

Reproduce the assessment on page 59. Have students write to show that they can apply their knowledge about controlling heat energy.

Note: Reproduce these picture cards to use with "Think about Controlling Heat" on page 52.

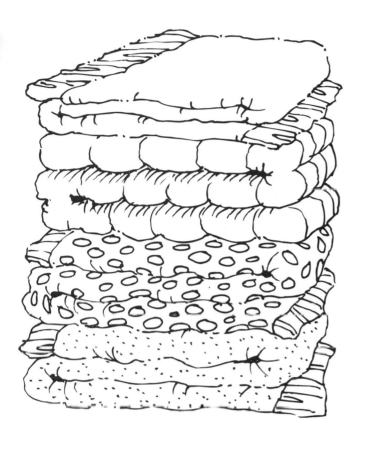

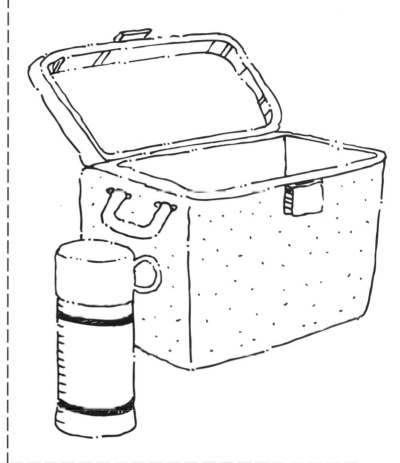

Note: Reproduce this poem to use with page 52.

We keep warm by keeping heat inside.

It's cold outside, but I'm staying warm.
I won't be bothered by the storm.

I have my mittens and my hat.
I have a new coat. How 'bout that?

I've extra socks and long underwear.
Let it get cold. I don't really care.

I'll wrap a muffler around my face
And keep my heat in this toasty space.

Energy: Light, Heat, & Sound • EMC 861

Meet Mrs. Check

Group Members _____

Keeping Heat in the Cup

This is how we will keep the water hot:

_____

_____

_____

_____

_____

Temperature	control	our experiment
at beginning		
after 5 minutes		
after 10 minutes		
after 15 minutes		

We showed that

_____

_____

_____

_____

_____

We could contain heat better if we

_____

_____

     Energy: Light, Heat, & Sound • EMC 861

Name _____

Keep It Hot!

Write to tell how to keep the heat from escaping in each different situation. Be sure to tell why your idea will work.

_____

_____

_____

_____

_____

_____

_____

_____

_____

Sound is energy you can hear.

Understanding Sound

Exploration 1 — A Sound Center

Set up a sound center contained in a box or crate. Provide bells, drums, rattles, and other simple musical instruments.

Ask students to describe the different sounds they make using the instruments and to explain how each sound is made.

This center is a great outdoor recess activity. Provide clipboards and pencils for recording information (reproduce the logbook form on page 4) and enjoy the purposeful play.

Exploration 2 — Sounds All Around

Listen inside and outside for sounds. List the sounds on a class logbook page. As you list the sounds have students tell what made the sound. You may want to take time to classify the sounds into groups. Have students develop the categories after reading over the list. For example, sounds might be categorized by source (sounds made by people, machines, or animals) or volume (sounds that are loud, soft, close, faraway.)

We heard loud sounds.

Recess bell
Car horn
Kids yelling

We heard soft sounds.

Clock ticking
Our own breathing

Summarize What Was Learned

• Discuss the idea that sound is energy that is heard.

• Summarize your discussion by writing a free-verse poem about sound using "ing" words.

Energy you can hear —
singing, laughing,
chirping, crying,
whispering, sweeping,
Sounds are energy you can hear.

Sound energy is created by vibrating objects.

Vibrations Produce Sounds

Creating a one-string "ukulele" to help your students see that vibrating objects produce sounds.

Materials

- rubber band
- ruler
- pencil

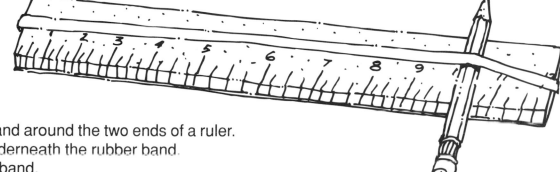

Steps to Follow

1. Wrap a rubber band around the two ends of a ruler.
2. Push a pencil underneath the rubber band.
3. Pluck the rubber band.
   What happens? What caused the sound?
4. Move the pencil and pluck again.
   Does the sound change?

Follow Up

Guide students to recognize that sounds were made when plucking the rubber band caused it to move back and forth (vibrate). The sound is higher or lower depending on the placement of the pencil.

Exploring Vibrations

Pairs of students will make a set of Super Listener Earphones and then use them to listen to the vibrations made by various objects.

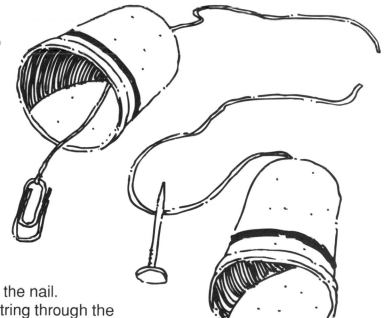

Making Super Listener Earphones

Materials (for each set)

- 2 paper cups
- 1 yard (1 meter) of string
- 2 paper clips
- nail

Steps to Follow

1. Make a hole in the bottom of each cup with the nail.
2. Cut the string in half. Put one end of each string through the hole in the bottom of each cup.
3. Tie each string end inside the cup to a paper clip.

Exploring Vibrations with the Earphones

Set up stations where the student pairs can take turns completing four tasks to find out about vibrations.

Materials

- slinky
- metal coat hanger
- fork
- spoon
- Listening to Vibrations task cards on page 63

Follow Up

- After all students have completed the four tasks, discuss their findings. Ask students:

    "Did the slinky make any noise before it was tapped?"
    "What about the hanger? the fork? the spoon?"
    "What was the same about all the sounds?"

- Record student observations on a class logbook page entitled "Listening for Vibrations."

Guide students to express the idea that when the objects were plucked or tapped there were sounds. The object had to start vibrating before the sound was audible.

Listening to Vibrations
Task 1

Stretch a slinky so that it is about 2 yards long.

Tie your earphones near the middle of the slinky.

Put both cups to your ears and listen.

Have your partner pluck one end of the slinky.

How does it sound now?

Switch jobs with your partner.

Listening for Vibrations

The slinky sounds got loud when Jamie tapped the end.

The super listener earphones worked like a stethoscope so I could hear the vibrations.

Listening to Vibrations
Task 1

Stretch a slinky so that it is about 2 yards long.

Tie your earphones near the middle of the slinky.

Put both cups to your ears and listen.

Have your partner pluck one end of the slinky.

How does it sound now?

Switch jobs with your partner.

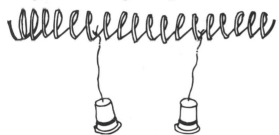

Listening to Vibrations
Task 2

Tie an earphone to each end of the hanger.

Put both cups to your ears.

Have your partner tap the middle of the hanger.

How does it sound?

Switch jobs with your partner.

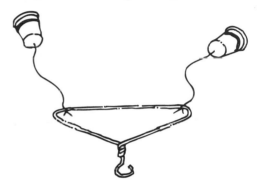

Listening to Vibrations
Task 3

Tie both of the earphone strings to the fork handle.

Put both cups to your ears.

Have your partner tap the tines of the fork.

How does it sound?

Switch jobs with your partner.

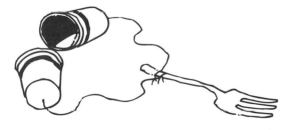

Listening to Vibrations
Task 4

Tie both of the earphone strings to the spoon handle.

Put both cups to your ears.

Have your partner tap the bowl of the spoon.

How does it sound?

Switch jobs with your partner.

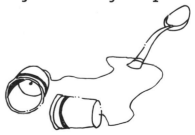

Energy: Light, Heat, & Sound • EMC 861

Sound travels at different speeds through different materials.

Exploring How Sound Travels — A Table Top Transmitter

Steps to Follow

1. As students listen closely, scratch on a desk or a table with your fingernail.
2. Ask students to describe the sound.
3. Have several children put their ears on the desk or table and scratch again in the same way.
4. Ask those students if there was a difference in the sounds.
   "Did the rest of the class hear a difference?"
   "What could have caused the difference?"
   (Sound moves faster through a dense material like wood or formica than it does through the air.)
5. Pair students so that each can scratch a solid surface while the other listens. The listener should first sit by the surface and listen, and then listen with an ear down on the surface.

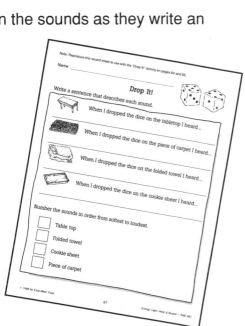

Have students speculate about what caused the difference in the sounds as they write an entry for their individual logbooks, using the form on page 4.

Exploring How Sound Travels — Drop It!

Materials

- wooden table top, square of carpet, folded towel, cookie sheet, some dice
- record sheet on page 67, reproduced for each student

Steps to Follow

1. Set up a center containing the material listed.
2. Pairs of students drop the dice on the four different surfaces.
3. Students describe the sounds that the dice make each time by recording their observations on the record sheet.

Follow Up

• When all students have completed the center activity, share their results. Ask them to think about why the sounds are different. Consider questions like these:

"If you were going to tap dance, which surface would you want?"
"If you didn't want to wake up a baby, which surface would you want in the hallway outside the baby's bedroom door?"
"If you were planning a math center that included a dice game, what could you do so that students working at the center would not disturb students doing seat work?"

• Explain that materials through which sound travels well are called **good conductors**. Materials through which sound travels poorly are called **poor conductors**. Discuss how the materials used in the exploration would be classified.

• Have students complete individual logbook pages using the form on page 4 to answer these questions:
"Does sound travel the same on all surfaces?"
"What might cause the difference?"

• Reproduce the record sheet on page 68. As a homework activity, students are to find six different materials where sound travels well and six materials where sound travels poorly.

When students return the sheets, create a class logbook page entitled "Good Sound Conductors" and "Poor Sound Conductors."

Ask why some materials are better conductors than others are. Guide students to see the connection between density and sound. They may even be able to explain that the molecules in a solid are closer together so that it's easier for the sound to move from one molecule to another.

Good Sound Conductors

stove top
water pipe
metal serving tray

Poor Sound Conductors

bed
pile of clothes
Dad's stuffed chair

Solids, liquids, and gases are all conductors of sound, but the speed of sound is different for each type of material. Most sounds that we hear are transmitted through the air. Sound waves travel much faster through solids and liquids than through gases because the molecules of solids and liquids are closer together.

Extension Activity — Tracking

You will need a playground ball.

Steps to Follow

1. Take students to the playground.
2. Move at least ten feet away and bounce a ball.
3. Ask students if they heard a sound when the ball hit the surface.
4. Now have students press one of their ears to the ground.
5. Bounce the ball again and ask students whether the sound was softer or louder than before.

Follow Up

Back in the classroom, discuss the result of the activity. Can students relate this to the previous explorations of how sound travels? Have they ever seen pictures of someone placing an ear to the ground in order to hear better? (Early trackers used this method to hear approaching people. They could feel the vibrations through the ground before they could hear them through the air.)

Name _____

Drop It!

Write a sentence that describes each sound.

When I dropped the dice on the tabletop I heard...

_____

When I dropped the dice on the piece of carpet I heard...

_____

When I dropped the dice on the folded towel I heard...

_____

When I dropped the dice on the cookie sheet I heard...

_____

Number the sounds in order from softest to loudest.

☐ Table top

☐ Folded towel

☐ Cookie sheet

☐ Piece of carpet

Name _____

Traveling Sounds

Look around your house. Tap different materials. Does the sound travel better in some materials than in others? Write down 6 of the materials where sound traveled well and 6 of the materials where sound traveled poorly.

Sound travels well in
these materials:

1. _____

2. _____

3. _____

4. _____

5. _____

6. _____

Sound travels poorly in
these materials:

1. _____

2. _____

3. _____

4. _____

5. _____

6. _____

Draw a good sound conductor.

Draw a poor sound conductor.

Sound can be controlled by changing the length of, or directing, sound waves.

Controlling Sound Exploration 1 — Using Megaphones

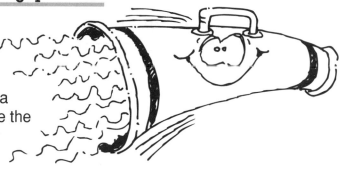

Invite a cheerleader or pep squad member to demonstrate a cheer using a megaphone.

Give students an opportunity to talk through a megaphone. Discuss what the megaphone does to a sound. (A megaphone makes sound louder because the sound waves are channeled in one direction, rather than spreading evenly in all directions.)

Controlling Sound Exploration 2 — Musical Bottles

Set up this experience as a center or use it as a demonstration.

Materials

- 4 identical glass bottles
- food coloring
- large pitcher of water

Steps to Follow

1. Add food coloring to the water in the pitcher.
2. Pour colored water into the bottles as shown.
3. Blow across the top of the bottles one at a time.
4. Describe the sounds that you hear.
   Is there a difference in the sounds?
   What causes the difference?
   Is this like anything else you know about? (Guide students to equate this demonstration with how wind instruments make sound.)

> Sounds become higher as the rate of vibration increases. The shorter the column of air, the faster the vibration and, thus, the higher the sound. The longer the column of air, the slower the vibration and, thus, the lower the sound. We call the highness or lowness of sound its pitch. Wind instruments change pitch by changing the length of the column of air.

Follow Up

1. Record student responses on a class logbook page entitled "We Can Control Sound."
2. Have students recall their experiences with the one-string "ukulele" (page 61). *(The pitch of the sound changed when the length of the rubber band changed.)* Invite a violinist to your classroom to demonstrate the way that pitch changes when the length of a violin string is changed.

Check for Understanding

Reproduce the worksheet on page 70. Show your students a toy xylophone. They will use what they know about controlling sound to answer questions about the sounds a xylophone makes.

Name _____

Xylophone Sounds

Color the highest note red.
Color the lowest note blue.
Put an **X** on the key that vibrates the fastest.
Put a ✓ on the key that vibrates the slowest.

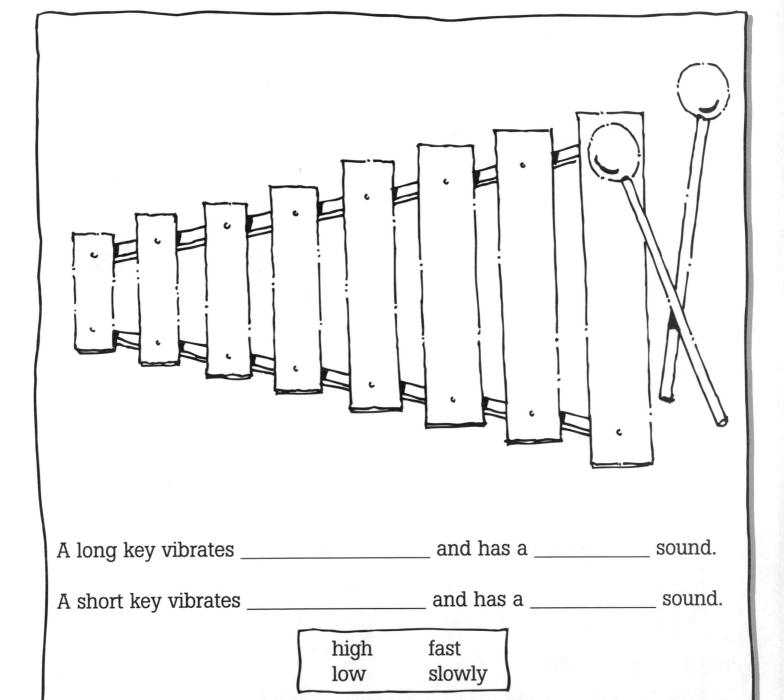

A long key vibrates _____ and has a _____ sound.

A short key vibrates _____ and has a _____ sound.

high	fast
low	slowly

Light, heat, and sound can move and change matter.

This unit began with the concept that energy can move and change things. You then explored three types of energy — light, heat, and sound — with your students. In this final section, students will explore how each of these types of energy can move or change matter.

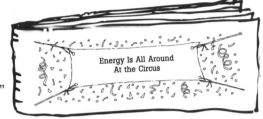

The unit ends with two summary activities:

1. a minibook on pages 77 and 78.
   After putting the book together and reading it, you may want your students to write their own "Energy All Around" book using the circus edition as a model. You might try "Energy All Around the School" or "Energy All Around the Playground."

2. an energy poster on page 79.
   Students show that they recognize what energy can do by pasting pictures from page 80 next to the correct energy statements.

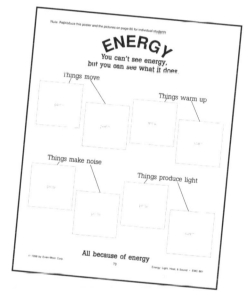

Light Energy Can Change Matter

Materials

- letter patterns on page 74
- 6" x 18" (15 x 45.5 cm) strip of colored construction paper
- tape
- logbook form on page 5

Steps to Follow

1. Cut out the letters.
2. Secure each letter to the construction paper with a single loop of tape. (The letters will be removed later in the project.)
3. If desired, cut some simple paper shapes from leftover paper and add them to the paper strip.
4. Tape the construction paper sign to a window where the sun will shine on it.
5. After a week, take the sign down and remove the letters and shapes.
6. Using the logbook form, describe the change that occurred. Tell about the energy that caused the change.

         Energy: Light, Heat, & Sound • EMC 861

Heat Energy Can Change Matter

Reproduce the simple recipe for making pancakes found on page 75. Post it at the cooking area. Under adult supervision, students will mix their individual batter and cook pancakes on an electric fry pan.

Ingredients

- flour
- cornmeal
- baking soda
- vanilla yogurt
- egg
- honey

Equipment

- tablespoon
- teaspoon
- small bowls
- spoon for stirring
- electric fry pan
- spatula

Hint: Beat up some eggs with a little water in a bowl or large cup. Students measure their tablespoon of egg from this container.

Follow Up

Discuss the changes that occurred during the cooking process.
Reproduce the logbook form on page 5 and have students record their observations.

Sound Energy Can Move Matter

Create coffee can vibrators to show that sound vibrations can move matter.

Materials

- balloon
- coffee can with both ends removed
- large rubber band
- sugar
- metal pan
- metal spoon

Steps to Follow

1. Cut a balloon and stretch it across the top of the open coffee can. Secure it with a rubber band.
2. Place a teaspoon of sugar in the center of the balloon.
3. Hold a metal pan close to the can and bang the pan with a spoon.
4. Discuss what happens. What made the sugar move? (The sound wave created by banging the pan caused vibration [movement] in the sugar.)

Explain a Change

This activity will allow students to show understanding of how energy can change matter.

To model the activity, make a transparency of page 76 and have students help you fill it in using the light and heat explorations on pages 71 and 72. Then brainstorm and list things students could do to change something by adding a form of energy.

Here are some possibilities for your list:
    make a baker's clay animal
    light a candle
    dry a wet cloth
    make toast for breakfast
    take a photograph

Divide students into groups and give each group a copy of page 76. They are to complete the sheet to explain a change of their choice.

Share the completed pages and bind them together to make an interesting nonfiction class book.

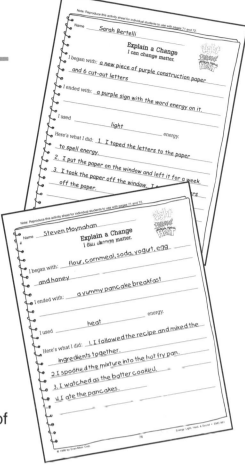

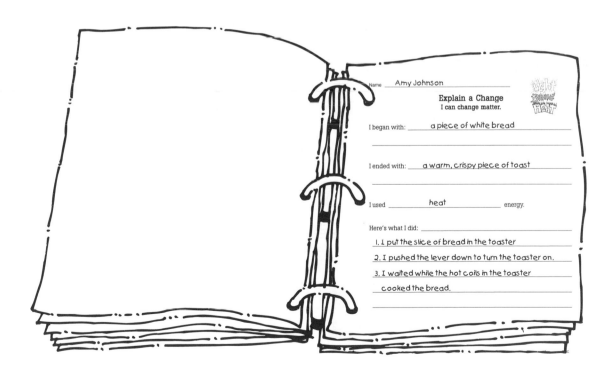

ENERGY

Note: Reproduce this recipe poster for use with the exploration on page 72.

Cornmeal Pancakes

Put in a small bowl:

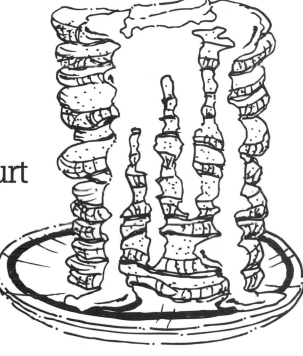

1 tablespoon of flour
1 tablespoon of cornmeal
a pinch of baking soda
2 tablespoons of vanilla yogurt
1 tablespoon of beaten egg
1 squirt of honey

Stir the ingredients together.

Spoon into lightly oiled fry pan heated to 375°.

Cook one side.

Flip the pancake and cook the other side.

Enjoy with butter and maple syrup.

Name _____

Explain a Change
I can change matter.

I began with: _____

_____

I ended with: _____

_____

I used _____ energy.

Here's what I did: _____

_____

_____

_____

_____

Energy Is All Around
At the Circus

Energy is all around us.

1

The light you see is energy.

2

The sound you hear is energy.

3

The heat you feel is energy.

4

Sometimes the energy is stored, waiting....

5

Sometimes the energy causes things to move and change.

6

Energy is all around us.

7

ENERGY

You can't see energy, but you can see what it does.

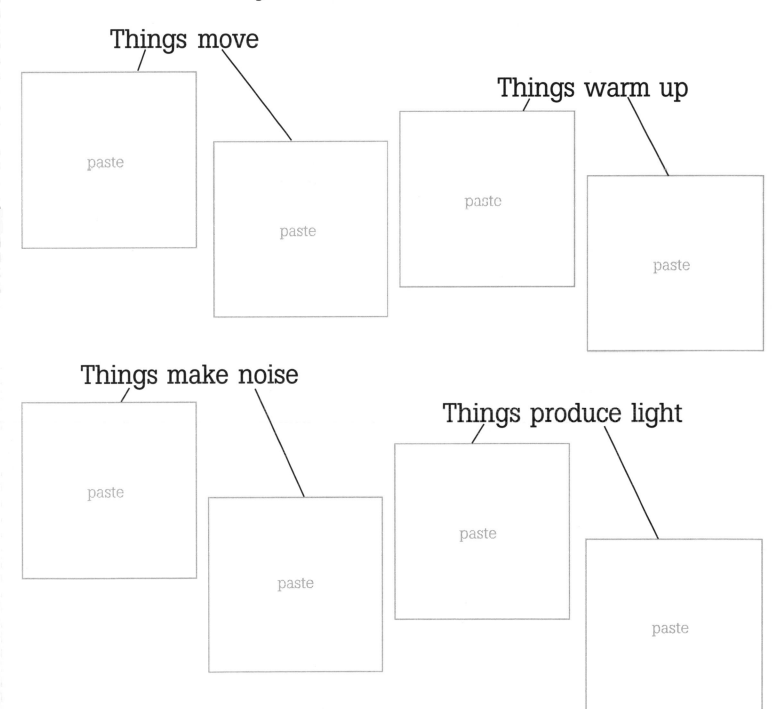

Things move

paste

paste

Things warm up

paste

paste

Things make noise

paste

paste

Things produce light

paste

paste

All because of energy

Cut out the pictures and paste them in the boxes to finish the poster.

Energy: Light, Heat, and Sound • EMC 861

EMC 861 • Energy: Light, Heat, and Sound

Cut out the pictures and paste them in the boxes to finish the poster.